MW00617312

CORY'S STORY

HOW ONE DOG CONQUERED EPILEPSY

SANDRA DeMERS

BOOK PUBLISHERS NETWORK

Book Publishers Network
P.O. Box 2256
Bothell • WA • 98041
PH • 425-483-3040
www.bookpublishersnetwork.com

10 9 8 7 6 5 4 3 2 1

Printed in the United States of America

LCCN 2010934506
ISBN10 1-935359-55-X
ISBN13 978-1-935359-55-5

www.corysstory.com

Front cover photo taken by Jayson DeMers

Back cover photo of Cory taken by Darrell Rude, owner of Positive Image Photography Studio, Anchorage, Alaska

Editor: Julie Scandora
Cover designer: Laura Zugzda
Typographer: Stephanie Martindale

DEDICATION

This book is dedicated with great fondness to Marion Mitchell in memory of her beloved Dalmatian, Kokopelli Mrs. Emma Peel CGC (April 28, 1993–March 20, 2007), as they were the team that we watched and opened the way for us into the world of proper canine nutrition. As a result of following them on that journey, Cory's seizures were gradually reduced and finally ceased, without his ever taking any anti-epileptic drugs. (www.canine-epilepsy.com)

CONTENTS

ACKNOWLEDGEMENTS

I want to thank my patient readers and Cory's followers who have waited almost a year for this book to be published, meanwhile reading about Cory on our Web site and sending him messages of encouragement and prayers for his recovery when he had spinal surgery in March 2010. Your support, love of animals, and the sharing of your stories about your own experiences with canine epilepsy have been deeply moving.

I also gratefully thank my son, Jayson, for creating the Web site and getting the word out to people all over the world about the miracle of Cory's full recovery from epilepsy. Although I wasn't happy when he said it, I have to thank him now for all the times he read the manuscript and said, "It's good, Mom, but it's not ready yet," and for all the excellent suggestions he made along the way. This book would not be nearly as good without everything he has done.

I must also thank my dear friend, Johanna Huhn, for sharing the journey with me, starting when we met at a place to get help for our epileptic dogs and continuing through her reading of the manuscript to give me the benefit of her keen eye for editing and on to double checking (and correcting!) my facts about canine epilepsy.

Finally, I fondly thank my cousin, Darrell Rude, who is a professional photographer, for generously allowing me to use photographs that he took of Cory over the years, both on the Web site and in this book

CORY'S STORY

Cory and Jayson on the lake beneath Mt. Adams. The boys loved water since the time they were puppies.

CHAPTER 1

THE TROUBLE BEGINS

I awakened to a glorious day in late July of 2000 without a cloud in the sky over our campground in southern Washington in the shadow of majestic Mt. Adams. To my delight, the lake was a sparkling emerald green; a detail we couldn't tell the night before as we had arrived after dark. Cory, our three-year-old yellow Labrador retriever, lifted his head and thumped his tail a few times, looking at me intently as if to say, "I'm ready when you are!"

Careful to get out of bed without waking Jay, who was still sleeping peacefully, Cory and I stepped outside to prepare for our morning walk. The pristine summer air in the cool morning breeze made me wonder if one could possibly feel any freer of the problems and worries that come with everyday life in the city, which we had left at home. I took a deep breath, tilted my head back, and let the sun warm my face.

Camping is, without any doubt, Cory's favorite activity, too. Eager to get the day started, Cory let out a little woof to snap me out of my early reveries and to remind me that I'd better get him fed before what was sure to be a big, fun day of swimming in the lake. I poured his kibble into his bowl and opened a can of Alpo to make it tasty, trying to be as quiet as possible so as not to disturb my husband, Jay, or Jayson, our son, who was sleeping in a nearby tent. Cory gobbled it up and looked at me with dancing eyes, as if to urge me to drink my hot cocoa faster so he could go swimming. I gulped the rest of it down, grabbed the tennis ball, and headed towards the lake with Cory bouncing like a dog on a pogo-stick beside me.

I threw the tennis ball for Cory into the lake to fetch for a good hour, and we returned to the motor home to find Jay and Jayson up for the day and getting ready for breakfast. Jay prepared breakfast and suggested that we all go out on the lake in our rubber Sevylor six-person raft. I wanted to go, but something about Cory gave me pause. I told them to go on and that I'd do the breakfast clean-up. As I went about my chores, Cory started to appear worried and clingy, a behavior I had never seen in him before. I was sitting in a lawn chair just outside our motor home with a book, which I was trying to read, with Cory lying at my feet, but I couldn't get into the book because I was becoming more and more aware that Cory was out of sorts. I wondered if Cory's mood related to a physical reaction to something in the water that made the color of the lake so emerald green. My internal alarm bells started ringing louder and louder as Cory's discomfort increased.

Suddenly Cory looked into my eyes with an expression at once both pleading and desperate. I watched in horror as his eyes rolled back in his head and he stood up on his hind legs. Before his body fell backwards to the ground, I had my arms around him to brace the fall. I had no idea what was going on. I screamed for help and kept my arms around Cory. His body convulsed violently to and fro. Thinking that he was having a heart attack, I did my best to apply CPR to his chest. I kept calling out and crying, and Cory's body kept twisting and writhing, and finally our fellow campers started to circle around me, summoned by my screams for help. They saw Cory and me, wrestling there in the dirt as I continued trying to give him CPR. One person said that my dog was obviously very old and at the end of his life. Through tears and clenched teeth as I held Cory's body on the ground, I said he had just turned three years old two months before. The "uh-oh squad," which consisted of about ten fellow campers, then offered up the collective opinion that Cory was having a seizure. I pleaded that someone go see if they could find my husband and son. Jay recalls that he was getting the raft and fishing poles ready to enter the lake when he heard someone calling his name. He paid no attention at first, thinking that the call was not intended for him. When he heard the words "Your wife needs you because your dog is having a heart attack," he and Jayson bolted up the hill.

They found me still on the ground, holding Cory in my arms with tears streaming down my face. The seizing had ended, but Cory was lying in my lap unable to move a muscle.

Jay picked Cory up and put him into the motor home. With no time to pack, we asked our camping neighbors to guard our belongings, and we took off for the nearest town. I was actually somewhat heartened that someone had suggested Cory was having a seizure instead of a heart attack because I knew that there were drugs available to manage seizures. I held Cory for the entire bumpy ride, praying that he would not die before we could get help. I could feel a slow heartbeat, but Cory's eyes were closed, and his body seemed otherwise lifeless. Saliva drooled out of his mouth and drenched my hands, face, and clothing, and I wondered silently if he could choke on it. At times, I could not even detect if he was still breathing.

With desperation and determination, Jay drove our motor home way too fast down the eighteen-mile washboard logging road that led to the nearest town, about an hour's drive from our campground. We did not care about the substantial damage done to our motor home on that drive; our only focus was on saving Cory's life. From time to time, Jay's eyes would meet mine in the rear-view mirror. Without speaking, we exchanged, "Is he still alive?" "Yes, just barely." I could not bring myself to turn and look behind me at Jayson, who was absolutely silent.

Chapter 2

I Won't Get the Dog!

Thirteen summers ago, Jayson was eleven and no longer needed day care, but Jay and I thought he would benefit from a companion outside of school hours. As a family, we decided a puppy would perfectly fill that void in the day. Like all boys, Jayson had always wanted one, and as his parents, we thought a puppy would keep Jayson away from the TV and video games in our absence as both Jay and I worked full time in downtown offices.

Jay took the lead and decided that a Labrador retriever would be the best dog for us because of the breed's temperament, intelligence, and versatile abilities. These attributes and more contribute to the selection of the Lab as the most popular breed for service dog for the blind or disabled and often as a tracking or bomb-finding dog for police work because of its keen sense of smell. Jay further decided that we would get a male dog and name him "Buck" or "Beau." Jay clearly had visions of pheasant hunting with his loyal canine companion ever vigilant at his side. "Why not a rescue dog?" I asked, feeling somewhat guilty about all the dogs in shelters that would make excellent candidates. Jay explained that he didn't want the dog to have any defects that would make it die an early or painful death, such as elbow or hip dysplasia, eye disorders, or some of the other diseases that you can't tell if you are getting into with a rescue dog. No, he wanted a perfect dog and was willing to pay for it.

Jay located the breeder on the other side of our state and found that he had a yellow male who was just about ready to go to a forever home. Jay proudly announced that we'd be getting our puppy that coming weekend. I couldn't believe it! Getting a dog *sight unseen*? I had envisioned going to the home of a breeder and watching the pups interact and finally choosing *the one* after several visits, which would allow us to get to know their personalities. But here was Jay, advocating that we travel far away to get a new family member without ever even seeing a photograph! I stomped my foot and said, "I **won't** get a dog without seeing it!" I stomped it again for good measure.

Jayson and Jay just looked at me.

Jay suggested that I call the breeder to get more information about the puppy. So I did, and I was told that the pup was the last yellow one left in the litter. We all had our hearts set on a yellow dog. So I reluctantly listened to what the breeder had to say. He said that the puppy's mother was a yellow Lab named "Josie" and his father was a black Lab named "Raider." He went on that Josie and Raider were pedigreed with both field and show champions as their ancestors. He added that he had papers to show the names of the ancestors and all the titles they had won. He finished by telling me that his dogs were certified to have no hip, elbow, or eye problems. I started to get interested.

We agreed that he would meet us halfway across the state, and if we didn't like the puppy, we would be under no obligation because he was delivering other pups from the litter to their new owners at the same time. He would just take the yellow pup back home if we didn't like him.

And so, we headed out that morning to meet our new dog, and I embarked on one of the most exciting days of my life, despite my concerns. We had arranged to meet at Rosso's U-Tote-Um, which is a small burger joint in Ellensburg, Washington, about a three-hour drive from our home in Seattle. The three of us sat, waiting on a picnic table, for over an hour, our excitement gradually turning to concern, wondering where they could be. Jay remembered that the breeder had mentioned he was delivering puppies to new owners at the same time, and he went to see if they were at the Ellensburg McDonald's (the other burger joint in the town). They were, so Jay came back and got Jayson and me.

The first moment I saw the yellow, five-and-a-half-week-old puppy, he had been drinking water from his little bowl in the back of the breeder's truck, resulting in a water spot on his face. I thought it was a rather unfortunate defect until the breeder noticed my expression, and with a flick of his finger, he dried the spot to reveal the cutest little fur-face I had ever seen. I immediately fell in love.

He has the most endearing little cowlick that runs vertically on his forehead, right between his eyes. Jay said that was where the mold must have cracked and a little bit escaped when God poured the Cory puppy in it to create him. Since Jay and Jayson never had any doubt about it from the beginning, we all knew without needing to say it aloud that we were going to be bringing him home with us.

CHAPTER 3

HOW CORY GOT HIS NAME

On the drive home, we marveled at the magnificent names on the Certificates of Pedigree for the puppy's ancestors, which the breeder had given to us, names like Waldorf's High Tech and Sunnyview's Abracadabra and Governor Woody's Best. It turns out the puppy's parents were actually named "Columbia's Golden Classic" and "Columbia's High River Raider." The breeder explained that it is common to give a pedigree name to a purebred dog and that the name of the kennel where the pup was whelped is often part of its name. His kennel was "Columbia's River Kennels." I pondered that on the drive home, and the name Columbia's Shining Son, came to me. The "Shining Son" referred to the puppy's yellow color and to the fact that he belongs to Jayson, our son. Jay and Jayson loved the name, and that is how he is registered with the American Kennel Club.

Jayson came up with the name "Cory" from a running back he admired at the University of Washington, which was fitting because the mascot for the team is the Huskies, a.k.a., "dawgs." Jay reluctantly let go of his vision of "Buck" or "Beau" and was a good sport about the name Cory.

If I look cute enough, they'll never suspect it was me when they find this thing shredded to pieces

Chapter 4

Cory's First Nights

We had already purchased a crate for Cory to sleep in and had set it up in Jayson's room. I added a sheepskin rug, a warm water bottle wrapped in a soft blanket, and an old-fashioned wind-up alarm clock that loudly tick-tocked. These were tricks I had been told would give the puppy comfort those first nights away from his mother and litter mates.

As Jayson's room was right next to ours, I could hear every time the puppy cried and Jayson dutifully got up and took him outside. This happened about fifteen times the first night. Jayson looked pretty tired the next morning, but that was nothing compared to how he looked on the second morning after another night of constantly interrupted sleep. Over breakfast, Jayson broke down and said to me, "Please, let's give him back!" I decided it would be best for both of them if we moved Cory's crate to a place in the house where no one could hear him, and he soon learned to sleep through the night. By the time Jayson returned to school in September, Cory was housebroken and able to sleep with Jayson on his bed. We had a pet door installed so that he could go out into our fenced yard as he needed.

It was only a matter of time before the princess's servant grew too big to control. But the princess never relinquished her throne.

CHAPTER 5

CORY GETS A LEASH

Every evening when we got home from work, Jay and I would take Jayson and Cory to a nearby park. Cory trotted along with us without the need for leash; he was very happy to have a pack to follow. We'd sit in a circle and, in turn, call out, "Cory, COME," to teach him that command. He learned quickly and was quite motivated by the treats he received when he arrived at the lap of the one that had called him. I fed him kibble from a large bag that pictured a healthy, glowing yellow Lab. The bag said the chow would provide him with 100 percent of his daily nutritional requirements, and I thought it was probably especially made for Labs. Cory ate with typical Lab passion for anything edible.

One evening on our nightly trip to the park, Cory's ears suddenly pricked up, and he bolted across the field, as if being chased by the Hounds of Hell. We watched with bewilderment as he barreled towards a young couple seated on the grass enjoying a picnic. With a leap that would make a high jumper proud, Cory dived and his little body disappeared completely into a bag of potato chips. The startled couple jumped up and looked at us as we rushed in to grab our puppy, who was chomping chips as fast as he could. As Jay pulled him out of the potato-chip bag, Cory managed also to inhale a big bite from the sandwich in the man's hand. With flaming faces, we muttered apologies and carried our bad boy to the car. Next stop that night was at our local pet store to purchase a tiny little collar and a leash.

Chapter 6

Cory Gets a Taste of Raw Flesh

My first trip with Cory to the grocery store was quite a learning experience. I bought a beef roast, carrots, and potatoes to make the evening meal and returned to the car with the sack of groceries. I needed to make a quick stop at Target, which is in the same parking lot. By the time I returned to the car, I found Cory with the entire roast in his mouth. I reached for him and said **"CORY, NO!"** to which he responded by grrrrrring and shaking his head furiously with the pot roast slapping either side of his head. I rolled my eyes and pulled the meat out of his mouth, which I tossed into a nearby garbage can, because everyone knows raw meat isn't good for dogs. I went back into the store to buy another beef roast for dinner.

CHAPTER 7

MOTOR-HOME CAMPING

When Cory was a few months old, we bought a used twenty-two-foot motor home. Our first trip was to Yellowstone Park. Although if I had known how dangerous the park is for a dog we would not have chosen it, we could do little once we were there. Cory learned to wait patiently in the motor home for us as we went on excursions, but he had the taste of freedom from swimming in lakes and rivers when it was safe for him to do so.

On the way back, we stopped in Montana to see the town on the Indian reservation where Jay was born. Since we'd been motor-home camping for a week, we decided to sleep one night in a motel where we could all get convenient showers.

We checked into a dog-friendly motel, which was situated along a major highway. On the far side of the highway was Flathead Lake. The day was sunny and warm, as it was late August, and the lake sparkled in the sun invitingly. Jayson was walking about outside, and I let Cory out of the room to join him. Suddenly Cory spied the lake, and he took off with a big grin on his face with thoughts of swimming on his mind. I panicked as Cory ran full speed toward the highway, screaming, "CORY NO," as I ran after him. My knees buckled, and I went down. I shut my eyes, feeling certain we were about to experience a tragedy. Then I heard Jayson yell at me, "Catch the ball!" I looked up, and Jayson threw an imaginary tennis ball at me. I caught it and ran into the motel room. Cory did a 180-degree turn in mid-stride and chased me into the room. I shut the door and trembled for at least an hour. Jayson was only eleven years old at that time, and I was so thankful for his quick thinking under extremely stressful circumstances.

Cory Gets a Scooter

Chapter 8

Cory Gets a Scooter

Cory's seemingly unlimited energy was no problem in the months where we could get him to water so he could swim. Although he didn't mind swimming in the winter, we couldn't go camping during those cold months, so getting him access to a lake or river where he could swim became increasingly difficult because we have strict laws in our state about dogs on beaches. Of course, there are a few off-leash parks where we could and did take Cory to get his exercise, but I think we were all getting a bit bored by going to the same places and doing the same thing every few days.

The first time I heard about Daphne Lewis's dog scootering invention, I was intrigued. I bought her book and thought that Cory and Jayson would enjoy that experience. I met with Daphne and told her about my dog and son, and she sold me the scooter and the special harness contraptions that they would need. I bought everything and gave them as a Christmas gift to Jayson and Cory.

After we unwrapped our gifts that Christmas, the first thing Jayson wanted to do was try out the scooter. We piled the kids (Jayson and Cory) and the scooter into the motor home and headed for the nearest elementary school playground, which had a large paved surface. We hooked Cory up to the gear and he and Jayson flew away, just as I had imagined. After a few rounds Jayson hopped off and offered me the next ride. I was ebullient as I stepped on the scooter and Cory took off. I felt as if I were behind a team of malamutes on the Alaskan Iditarod trail. After my first few moments of experiencing the thrill of the ride, I began wondering how to slow the ride down. I applied the brakes. Although the scooter came fully equipped with brakes, the same as you would find on a bicycle, it had one difference: a bike stops when you brake, but a yellow dog full of joy and energy does not.

My braking resulted in the immediate stop of the scooter with Cory still pulling at full force, which flipped me high into the air. I did an aerobatically impressive somersault before I came down with a humiliating crash onto the playground. I landed on my left wrist and knew right away from the pain and the searing flash of nausea that things were not good. A trip to our local ER confirmed that I had broken a few bones in my left wrist.

I counted my blessings because I am right handed and was, for the most part, able to continue my work in my capacity as the senior paralegal at the law firm where I work. I went to a hand-and-wrist specialist who told me I was lucky to have barely escaped surgery to repair my broken bones.

Jayson and Cory continued their enjoyment of the scooter and spent many afternoons in nearby Lincoln Park, flying among the trees on the paved paths. I watched them with envy, but I had learned that dog scootering was not meant for me.

We never had any luck slowing down this kind of determination.

CHAPTER 9

MAKE THAT TWO
BROKEN WRISTS

As a member of our local swim and tennis club, Jayson had done very well in tennis that season and had advanced to the finals. The rest of his family, Jay, Cory, and I, went to watch his performance. We had Cory on his leash, and he behaved himself, being very mellow as Jay and I cheered our boy on. I was holding Cory's leash in my right hand, and I was so intent on the match that I missed an errant tennis ball that was hit out of the court by the team practicing in the opposite tennis court. But the ever tennis-ball vigilant Cory did not miss that ball coming over the fence and into his realm of catchability. He morphed from a mellow dog watching his boy in a tennis match to a tennis-ball obsessed dog in less than a heartbeat. Before I could even see the tennis ball sail over the fence, I had been jerked onto the concrete with what was left of Cory's leash in my right hand. The pain that seared through my wrist was confirmed as another break by my next visit to the ER. Now I had had both of my wrists broken within five months.

As my wrists were healing, I also had the unfortunate experience of Cory's head hitting me in the face one morning while we were playing, which resulted in a very obvious black eye. One of my co-workers gave me a key to her apartment and told me to use it anytime. Instantly understanding that she thought I was being abused by my husband, I tried my best to convince her that all of my recent breaks and bruises were attributable to my dog. She wasn't buying it and always looked daggers at Jay at our holiday parties.

Yes, Cory used to take US for walks.
We could only try to keep up.

Chapter 10

Cory Joins Cub Scouts

Jayson joined Cub Scouts when he was in second grade, and Jay and I became very active in it as well. By the time Cory came into our lives, Jayson had advanced to become a Webelos. We went on many excursions with the boys, filling our motor home with as many Scouts as we had seatbelts. Getting a ride with us was highly desired by the boys as we had a refrigerator, which could keep their sandwiches and drinks cool, and a table on which they could play Pokemon. Cory loved being part of the little-boy energy and managed to scoot the boys over enough so he could get up on the seats with them and peer at the cards. We involved him in every Boy Scout activity that we could, and with a green official Boy Scout neckerchief tied around his neck, he was accepted by the boys as one of them.

One afternoon, the boys were playing capture the flag in the field where we were having an overnighter, as we called them. Cory, of course, was having a great time running around the field with them. Jayson got a bit frustrated from time to time when Cory would give his position away, which anyone could tell by the way his tail would wag excitedly when he sniffed in Jayson's general vicinity. I don't know how he got it into his head actually to capture the flag himself, but I looked up when I heard a commotion to see Cory with the flag in his mouth, playing the keep-away game that he loved to do with sticks and tennis balls, being chased round the field by all the Cub Scouts, who badly wanted to win the game.

We also took the Scouts to the beach at the Washington Coast, where the boys and Cory would play hide and seek in the sand-dunes or run with kites trailing overhead high in the sky. On the hikes over mountain trails, he was actually appreciated by the younger Scouts who did not want to carry some of their gear, as Cory had a saddle-bag in which he loved to carry water bottles, candy bars, and other essential Boy-Scout supplies. Cory loved to race ahead of everyone on the trail and then turn about and trot back towards us as we made our way forward on the trail, making sure every single person was in line and moving forward. He'd keep this up until we'd arrive at our destination, so he traveled at least twice the distance as did the rest of us. If we met other dogs along the trail, Cory would not interfere with them at all. And he would come to me with a look on his face that I understood if he needed me to take his water bottle out of his saddle-bag so he could have a drink of water.

With enough speed, long enough wings and a perfectly vertical tailfin, Cory was sure he could learn to fly just like those darned elusive birds.

CHAPTER 11

BOWLING FOR BABIES

In Cory's first summer when we were camping on the Washington Coast by Forks, we decided to spend that day at the Sol Duc River, which was actually the confluence of two rivers. Near the beach where we set up our blankets, the water, although deep, was calm. On that hot August day, a rope swing over the calmer waters was very popular. Out further, about 120 feet away, the river was still very deep but moving swiftly. We had enjoyed hours at our spot on the riverbank with a blanket spread out for the Cory puppy (who had not yet learned how to swim). We would take turns dipping his little body into the water while we supported him with our hands so he could get used to the feeling of being in water. At this age, his puppy-velvet fur coat lacked the insulating and oily water-repellant properties, so he got cold easily. Shivering, he got a rub-down in a towel, and we laughed about how it was only a matter of time before our frightened, frozen little puppy would, like all of his proud ancestors, fall in love with the water.

Suddenly, I noticed that Jay's attention was focused on the river. I saw him exchange an intense look with another man who was also on the riverbank with his family. The two of them ran and jumped in at the same time, leaving Cory, Jayson, and me wondering what was going on. They swam with great energy and purpose out to the more turbulent part of the river while I struggled to keep Jayson from swimming after his father. Once I succeeded, he and I noticed the two people in the river that the men were swimming towards. The man who had jumped in with Jay grabbed one of them, and we watched from afar as Jay seemed to be tussling with the other one. I was really not aware of what was going on, although I was concerned.

Jay is an Eagle Scout, who got his lifeguard certification through Boy Scouts of America when he was fourteen years old. Although he never worked as a lifeguard, he had three prior experiences where he was the first responder in a life-and-death situation, and his training had prepared him well to handle each of them. Until that day, he had saved one life in those three situations. On this day, he recognized that two people in the river were in some kind of serious trouble. Both young women from the nearby town of La Push, they had been playing on the rocks near that fast-moving area of the river, and the current had caught them and pulled them off the rocks. The man who jumped into the river with Jay was the uncle of one of the girls, and he was able to get her to the safety of the riverbank, possibly because his niece knew and trusted him.

Jay was left with the young woman who did not know him and who was terrified into a blind panic. By the time he got to her, she had gone under water three times and was gasping for air. As she saw him swim towards her, with her dark eyes dilated with fear, she tried to climb up onto Jay, which pushed him under water. Using his lifeguard training skills, Jay spun her body around and grabbed her pony-tail in his right hand while he put his left hand around her chest and said to her firmly that if she did not stop struggling he would drown her. With those magic words, all of the fight went out of her, and she went catatonic.

Jay was able to swim against the current to get to a place on the riverbank where other people pulled the girl up out of the water.

Jay swam back to us and asked one of the kids on our beach if he could borrow a rubber flotation device, which he took over to the other side where he had left the girl. He got her to get onto the inflatable mattress, and he ferried her across the river to where we were and delivered her to her waiting friends. Numb from shock, she was unable to speak as Jay brought her back to our side of the river, or even to her friends once Jay got her safely to them.

The next day, we were walking on Rialto Beach and were approached by strangers who had watched the entire rescue operation the day before. They said that the girl had been taken to the local hospital in Forks to be treated for shock. I was able then to contact the hospital to check on how she was doing and was told that she had been treated and released. Anxious for more information, I somehow got her name. After some amateur detective work, I was able to locate her mother, who told me that Jay had saved her daughter's life that day. She said her daughter was not a strong swimmer, and she had become exhausted when her friend (a non-swimmer) got caught in the current and tried to cling to her to keep from drowning.

At that time, Jay was a recruiter for Boy Scouts (he moved to that position from Cub Master of Jayson's Cub Scout pack when Jayson became a Boy Scout), and so, as an active member of Boy Scouts, Jay was awarded the National Medal of Honor, the most prestigious award given by that organization, for saving a life by risking your own life.

This rescue made a huge impression on both Jayson and Cory. Several years later, Jayson also got his BSA lifeguard certification one summer when he was at Boy Scout Camp. He was the only non-adult that summer to participate in and achieve that certification, while all the other boys worked on merit-badge requirements. About the time Jayson achieved his BSA lifeguard certification, Cory, wanting to be with his boy at all times, also became an extremely strong swimmer. It was inspiring to watch the two of them swim together, far out into lakes or rivers. The faster the currents in rivers, the more Cory enjoyed it. He quickly taught himself just where to enter and exit a fast-moving river so that he could enjoy a Disneyland-like joy ride, grinning at everyone with delight as his webbed feet capably navigated the ferocious currents. He learned where the currents would allow him to get back to the shore so he could trot back to his starting place and go again. These shows would often attract people who had never before seen a dog as strong and capable as Cory, happily maneuvering in what would, in most any other circumstances, be extremely dangerous for any human or animal.

During that same trip to the coast, we were walking along Rialto Beach, enjoying the beauty of yet another day. Cory ran ahead of us, grinning broadly. Everyone we walked by smiled at the happy scene of the shiny yellow puppy running free … until I noticed a family with a small toddler coming towards us on the beach. Cory loves children. Oh, no, he wouldn't, would he? Yes, he hit fourth gear as he sprinted down the beach with the three of us running after him hollering, "Cory, NO!" Unhappily, by the time we caught up with him, Cory and the toddler were both sprawled on the beach, the baby looking dazed. We apologized profusely to the baffled parents and collected our wayward pup and got out of there. Although no harm was done, we decided that even on a beach it would be a good idea to keep Cory on a leash, lest he get it in his mind that bowling for babies was his newest favorite game.

Cory did eventually learn to fly, perfecting the Superman form as shown here.

CHAPTER 12

A MOST UNUSUAL REACTION

We continued to do a lot of camping in our motor home, although after Yellowstone, our trips were usually limited to just three or four days at a time, and we pretty much stayed in Washington. Cory's love of camping and swimming was infectious and he made us laugh all the time. By the next summer, with over twelve months behind him, he had grown into a strong, muscular being with unlimited energy. He would get a running start and then jump off a platform, planing his body like Superman flying through the air, before hitting the water. He would do that all day without ever tiring.

Then came the evening at Rimrock Lake in Eastern Washington. Cory had been swimming all day, running up and down a steep slope to chase a tennis ball into the lake. It was growing dusk, and Jay started our campfire. Suddenly Cory's body went rigid, as if he had turned to stone. He stood there with his eyes unfocused and drool running out of his mouth in a line to the ground. Alarmed, I touched him and tried to get him to respond. "Come on, boy!" I said with concern. "What's the matter?" He would not move. After a few moments I grabbed the cell phone and got information to connect me with a veterinary clinic in the nearest town. A nice lady veterinarian listened to my report and said, "Congratulations! You have just worn your dog out for the first time!" And sure enough, not long after, Cory snapped back to his self. The next day, he was full of the same energy and enthusiasm as ever before.

CHAPTER 13

TRAINING

When wearing his leash, Cory constantly pulled us, and often he pitted his very strong will against ours, so we enrolled Jayson and Cory as a team into obedience training. They sailed through beginning and intermediate classes and were ready to tackle the advanced one. The purpose of the advanced class is for the dog to earn the title of Canine Good Citizen, or CGC. It is a title that can be put after the dog's name, the same as a person does who has achieved a title through a degreed educational program. Dog owners covet the title because both the dog and the human have to work very hard together in order to pass all of the requirements.

Cory loved the training classes and was a model student. In class, that is. As he walked on leash in a circle with all the other dogs, he never pulled, as he invariably would do the minute he was out of class. But under the guidance of the trainers, our ability to communicate with Cory increased to the point of all of us having abundant confidence with him. Most quickly, "training" became to Cory a beloved word that meant we were about to have special time together where he would get endless treats and be able to exchange important information.

We did not restrict training with Cory to the actual sessions we attended; we also extended it to every chance we had. As a result, each of us can be proud that we contributed something valuable to Cory's repertoire. In addition to responding to the commands *sit, stand, down,* and *stay,* Cory learned to wait while one of us would hide a toy and then return to him and say, "Go find!" which would blast him off as if launched by a rocket through the house using his keen sense of smell to locate the hidden object. He also learned to get our shoes or slippers (a heavenly treat at the end of a day in high heels) and to *circle,* which required that he turn in a circle in front of the person giving the command. (This one came in very handy in the days when Cory did scootering, to get his harness untangled.)

Cory is always happiest when he is with us as an interacting being. As a result of all of the time we spent together training *him,* he trained *us* to learn what he wants to communicate, like, "Hey guys, I'm really hungry" or "I need water" or "Let's play ball!" or "Let's go swimming!!!!" or, even, "I need to go nigh-nigh" (bed time). My favorite was when he was able to communicate, "I cannot contain my joy to be with you guys under these stars, around this campfire!" Like Cory, I don't want any of this life we have made together ever to end.

In addition to learning verbal commands, Cory mastered all of the hand signals that were taught at the same time the verbal commands were taught. Cory loved to put on shows for people when we were out camping or for our family and guests at our home. Within minutes of a guest's arrival at our home, Cory would be invited to show off all of his training as a way to bring positive attention to him and his abilities and to keep him from jumping on people or otherwise being marginalized from the human interaction.

Jayson and Cory did work hard in their classes, and although I wasn't sure if they were ready, they signed up to take the CGC exam on a Saturday, which happened to be Halloween that year. Jayson was then thirteen, and Cory was not yet two and a half. The dogs were paired up with their owners or handlers as teams. I watched with increasing hope as they made it through test after test. The forum was a large indoor arena and at least 150 people were there that day to see if they could make the grade. As soon as a dog failed any one of the requirements, the team had to stop. I noticed that every person with a dog there for the test was an adult, except for Jayson. The rigorous test went on and on for hours. The last requirement had the handler give his dog's leash to a stranger, tell the dog to stay, and walk away (behind a wall where the dog couldn't see him). The point was that the dog could not freak out and had to wait calmly with the stranger for the three minutes, which seemed an eternity to those of us watching.

Many dogs who had made it through the day with their handlers at their sides could not accept being abandoned by their human teammate, but Cory did great. When he was reunited with Jayson he grinned broadly and wagged his tail furiously in relief. I was smiling too until I saw that Cory did the little Cory wiggle which meant he had to pee. "Uh oh," I thought and right then the judge pointed at Cory and said "Canine Good Citiz—" and Cory let it go on a traffic cone set up in the arena. In front of everyone. The arena got very still and very quiet. Any dog that urinated or defecated during the test was automatically out. We all waited, holding our collective breath. The judge thought about it for a while and finally made the decision that Cory had peed after the completion of the test, not during it, so he was awarded his CGC—and everyone let out a great collective sigh of approval.

We decided to get into Agility Training next, and Cory again took to it with enthusiasm. He learned to go through tunnels, jump through hoops, and even walk along a balance beam high above the ground. We were not interested in competition; we just had fun learning new things with our dog. Jay trained Cory to get the newspaper from the top of our driveway every morning, a job he still does with pride. Labrador retrievers especially need to have jobs to do in order to be happy. And I am very happy when Cory does his job, especially on those mornings when it is pouring rain here in Seattle and I see Cory's shining eyes and wagging tail come into the house with the newspaper in his mouth, as our carrier drops it up at the top of our driveway, which is a far enough walk that I'd certainly get drenched if I had to get the paper myself.

OK, maybe you were right — I shouldn't have eaten those two
pumpkin pies. Now can you help me get out of here?

Chapter 14

Food Thief

But no matter how much training he got, Cory has always had a weakness for anything even remotely edible, and we have never been able to trust that any food (with the possible exception of lettuce) is safe around him. Before we figured this out, however, we suffered the consequences, such as what we call the pumpkin pie incident. Jayson loved pumpkin pies so much that he learned to make them, and they turned out really good. By our second Thanksgiving, Cory had reached his full height, and we knew that he could see up onto our kitchen counters. We knew he could see up there but we did not yet know how easily he could getup there. We learned that he had achieved that ability when Jayson put his pie on a rack to cool, fairly close to the front of the counter top. Jayson left the kitchen for a while and returned some time later to find Cory licking the pie plate clean. Jay went out and bought a new pumpkin pie from the grocery store, and I put it way back on the kitchen counter, feeling certain it was safe this time. I, myself then had Jayson's experience of returning to the kitchen to find Cory, with his tail wagging this time with all-out glee, licking the pan where the pumpkin pie had been. I said, "Oh, Cory!" and he burped.

Cory became a menace to our guests about that time, in that he would sniff out any snacks they brought and ferret them out of purses and suitcases left unattended. On one memorable visit, my elderly mother, whose purse was often scavenged by Cory because she did not want it to be far from her reach, decided that his name should be "Cory **No!**" I really wanted my mom to like Cory, but it never happened. She would watch him run through all of his tricks, which he could do with either verbal or silent hand signals (a show that impressed everyone else who saw it), and she'd sadly shake her head and declare that until we trained him to leave food (and anything else smelling remotely yummy) alone, he was a scoundrel.

I really tried! I felt like Wile E. Coyote laying traps for the Roadrunner in my schemes to dissuade Cory from stealing food. One time, I went so far as to string empty tin cans together along the kitchen countertop with a nice piece of steak tied to the end of the string. I left the kitchen and hid where I could still see as Cory entered the kitchen and quickly smelled the delicious treat, and although when he got it and pulled the string all the cans came tumbling down on him and made an awful noise, Cory was only momentarily surprised and then wagged his tail happily as he swallowed his prize.

I searched the Internet and found a tip that worked for us ever after—non-deadly mousetraps! I bought five or six small mousetraps at a nearby hardware store and set them up on the kitchen counter around a tasty steak. I left the kitchen and eventually heard a mousetrap snap, and Cory never again stuck his nose anywhere near a mousetrap. It is so simple to pop them out of a drawer in the kitchen and arrange them around whatever you want to protect. The first time my sister from Alaska visited me, the look on her face when she saw the mousetraps on my kitchen counter was priceless. I understood in a flash that she thought I had a big mouse (or even rat!) problem and that she was seriously considering checking into the bed and breakfast up the street.

CHAPTER 15

WELCOME TO THE WORLD OF CANINE EPILEPSY

This brings me back to that most glorious day in late July of 2000 when Cory had just turned three and had his first epileptic seizure, which I described in the opening pages of this book. We finally arrived at the tiny town of Troutdale and pulled into the parking lot of a veterinary hospital to which locals had directed us. Jay jumped out of the motor home and noted a sign on the door that said the staff was at lunch. He pounded on the door, and when it opened, he exclaimed we had a life and death emergency. They immediately became the professionals we needed them to be and stood by as Jay opened the passenger door on the motor home, ready to transfer Cory onto a gurney. Cory's ears went up at the familiar sound of the door rolling open, and he jumped out of my arms and ran down the stairs of our rig. He then proceeded to pee on their planters of flowers near the entrance door for at least three minutes and grinned up at us like an imp. The veterinarian and his assistants all watched Cory, who appeared to be a normal, ebullient three-year-old dog whose problem in life seemed to be that his owners had not allowed him to pee for several days. I stammered out what had happened as best I could, and the vet took Cory in for an exam.

He said that his heart and vitals were all perfect and explained that what had happened was most likely a grand mal seizure. He said we would know for sure if it ever happened again. I asked about getting drugs, and the vet said that would be a decision to be made by Cory's regular veterinarian. So, feeling as if our world had tipped upside down and then back upright again, we returned to the campground.

Cory was thrilled to swim in the lake (although I insisted that he be tethered to his long leash), and other campers came and told us how happy they were that Cory was still alive. Not only was he alive, he was the picture of health! I, on the other hand, was a bit of a mess for the rest of the weekend, remembering every searing detail of the seizure and my helplessness as Cory and I were rolling in the dirt as I tried to give him CPR. I could not connect my emotions of painful loss with the fact that we had him back again, as if it were all a bad dream. My bad dream, that is, not Cory's. He enjoyed every moment of the rest of that weekend, which was so beautiful. Dogs have a wonderful blessing of living in the present moment and enjoying what is. They don't fret about what happened a few moments ago, nor do they worry about what might be tomorrow.

Trying to incorporate those dog lessons into my being as much as possible, I started taking a lot of photographs. One of them was of Mt. Adams reflected in the lake. When the photograph was developed, it was nearly impossible to tell when it was upside down, as the reflection in the water came out as clear as the mountain itself. Many years later, we hired an artist to paint that photograph onto tile, and we had it installed in the shower/tub area of the bathroom in our home as a way of keeping alive that memory of a day that had such a profound impact on our family's life.

We hoped that Cory would not have another seizure, but not even two months after the first grand mal, he did. We took Cory to his regular vet in Seattle and explained about the two seizures he'd had, and we had a full work-up done. Every test came back negative, which meant that Cory had no brain tumor, no thyroid levels off, absolutely nothing physical that could explain why he was having seizures. So he was diagnosed as having idiopathic epilepsy, and we were advised to keep track of the seizures to see how often they were and if we could determine any possible triggers. I, of course, became the appointed seizure-keeping secretary.

CHAPTER 16

KING OF THE PARK

We started taking Cory to off-leash parks when he was still a puppy. Once he got over his original curiosity about other dogs, he started learning how to catch a Frisbee. After he reached his full size and maturity, I noticed that when we'd arrive at the park, the other dogs would naturally gravitate to him. Cory would enter the park with his tail held high and his eyes full of fun, and he would allow all the other furry kids to come over and sniff him, like a king permitting his court to attend to him. He always had quite the following, as if the other dogs saw Cory as their leader, or at least the one they thought was the most fun to hang around with. Even dogs otherwise engaged with their caregivers would get distracted from their play and join the gang of Cory's followers. I have always loved it that, even if off his leash, Cory would stay right with his humans and was never tempted to stray (once he got over bowling for babies and sprinting for food). I used to think that Cory would have been a top athlete if he had been human because of his quickness, agility, and endless stamina. But his favorite game, no doubt, would have been football. His intensity on the toy, be it a Frisbee or a tennis ball, allowed him no time to pay any attention to his fellow canines, so the routine was that we'd throw the toy for him and he would weave and dodge and even jump over all the dogs that just wanted to chase after him in order to be as close to Cory as they could get. Cory soon mastered the game of catching the Frisbee and would delight other dog owners by getting lots of air and impressive stretches when jumping for it.

I admit to feeling a strong sense of pride in having a dog that not only looks beautiful but that you can communicate with so easily. We were the envy of frustrated dog owners at the off-leash parks who would call for their dogs to leave ours alone, only to be ignored. I secretly laughed as one lady, red in the face, chased her little terrier around the park. Her terrier chased Cory, she chased the terrier, and I thought of the children's chant, "Ring around the rosy, ashes, ashes, we all fall down!" as her dog scooted away from her and she lost her footing and went splat in a muddy area near the watering stations.

We never have to raise our voice to get Cory's attention as he is so tuned into us, especially when we are engaged with each other doing something we all love to do. That pride, for me, dissolved into shame the first time Cory had a seizure in West Crest Park, the off-leash park near our home. Jayson and I had taken Cory to West Crest on that lovely summer day, looking forward to fresh air and exercise. We'd been playing for about a half hour when Cory suddenly stopped chasing the ball, and his eyes became unfocused. He staggered a few steps and collapsed. I suddenly felt that if I dared to look down I would see that all of my clothes had become invisible, so intense was my sense of vulnerability and shame. As I ran to Cory's side, I felt panic that the other dogs would attack him while he was seizing. I knew that animals will sometimes attack, instinctually try to weed out the weak among them or, perhaps, only trying to harm the silent monster that has a dog in its grip. I called to Jayson to help me by keeping the other dogs away, and he did a good job of it by telling people to help us by putting their dogs on their leashes for a few minutes. Thankfully, everyone either complied, or those that didn't understand what was going on simply took their dogs in another direction. That is one of the most frightening aspects of epilepsy in a dog, when the seizure hits and other dogs are nearby. This happened quite a few times during the years when Cory had seizures, not just at the off-leash park but also at the lakes where we'd often camp, where all of our fellow campers let their dogs off leash to play in the water.

I kept a written journal of every seizure Cory had in my presence or that I was told about. As I look over that record, I see that I talked a lot about pre and post ictal, where "ictal" means pertaining to a seizure. These terms refer to unusual attitudes by Cory either before or after a seizure, such as his acting worried or clingy. The period that precedes a seizure is also called the prodromal period, or aura. Although most of Cory's seizures hit without warning, some he could sense were coming, and he would run to me and lie against my legs or down at my feet. Of course, once I learned that these were prodromal symptoms, I would respond. I learned about how many animals get immediate comfort from Rescue Remedy, which is sold in every vitamin or health food store I've ever been in. This remedy has been known to relieve stress from such events as a visit to the vet or even for grooming. I bought lots of bottles and had one in my purse, one in the kitchen cabinets, one in our motor home, and one in my pocket wherever I went. Often I was able to get to the Rescue Remedy in time for it to make a marked difference in the intensity and duration of the seizure. On the day that Cory had his seizure in West Crest Park, I see from my journal that I did not have Rescue Remedy with me. That was the last time I went anywhere without it.

My seizure record kept track of Cory's seizures by date, time, whether he had any pre or post ictal, what exercise he'd had, and what phase the moon was in. He had quite a few seizures about the time of a full moon. In fact, Cory's last seizure, on May 22, 2005 at about eight in the evening, was on the eve of a full moon. I noted that afterwards I gave him preservative-free vanilla ice cream with honey on top, in order to help his body recover more quickly. The massive neural and physical activity during a seizure releases hormones and consumes glucose, which the ice cream and honey help to replace.

I later came to understand that the first seizure Cory had was actually at Rimrock Lake when he stood statue still with unfocused eyes and drooled. I only learned that because I wanted to educate myself about canine epilepsy and found help when I joined canine-epilepsy.com, a domain co-owned and hosted by Marion Mitchell, who was seeking to connect with others who had epileptic dogs.

CHAPTER 17

CANINE-EPILEPSY.COM

Marion's own dog, a show-quality, beautiful female Dalmatian named Emma, had epilepsy and had gone through absolute hell, as her seizures were frequent and severe. Marion kept up a blog, describing Emma's seizures. One of the things we owners need to do is describe the seizures in every detail to someone who cares because each one of them takes a part of us with them in terms of the pain, helplessness, and isolation we feel. Marion's site offered each of us that chance in addition to the fact that she had acquired a panel of extremely well-respected veterinarians who published the latest findings in the scientific world about canine epilepsy on her Web site. There I was able to share my stories and read about other people's experiences. At the end of our posts, after our signatures, we all began sharing every detail about what we fed our dogs, what anti-epileptic drugs they were on, if any, and what supplements we gave them. I learned from people who tried the various anti-epileptic drugs (AEDs) what the side-effects could be and how in some cases the dogs on AEDs faced other, equally frightening side-effects and shortened life expectancies. I immersed myself into the world of canine epilepsy and made friends with other human companions of "epis," as we called our dogs. I saw that some dogs would not survive without AEDs because the seizures were coming more often and, in some cases, clustering together. I began to feel as if I was running out of time for Cory because his seizures were also starting to come more frequently.

I began to see regular positive postings from those who tried homeopathy instead of anti-epileptic drugs and especially from those who started feeding a raw, species-appropriate diet. When we wrote about our experiences, we often could not bear to write the word "seizure" as it had too much of a negative impact on ourselves as well as each other. We spoke about "it" either in whispers, calling a seizure simply "s," or "the monster," as if we were collectively afraid that if we said the word "seizure" we would bring it into our reality. This experience made me understand the phrase, "speak of the devil," which refers to the common phenomenon of saying someone's name only to have the person appear moments later.

One day Marion Mitchell, herself, posted that she had tried everything for Emma, and she felt she had nothing to lose by trying her on a raw diet. She consulted a canine nutritional expert and was told how to feed Emma a diet that would mirror as closely as possible what a dog would eat in the wild. That would be small prey such as chickens and rabbits or even deer and other prey which can be brought down when wolves hunt together as a pack. Marion shared that information with all of us, and to my amazement, Emma's seizures quickly came under control. Over time, Marion was able to adjust Emma's anti-epileptic drugs so that she was able gradually to reduce the drugs, and Emma regained her clarity and her spirit of adventure. The other dogs owned by Marion had viciously attacked Emma on numerous occasions during her seizures, similar to what we had experienced with Cory in dog-run areas. But once Emma started eating raw chicken and other raw meaty bones, she regained her place of authority in her dog pack with the regency of a queen. That did it for me. I decided that before I put Cory on any drugs we were first going to try homeopathy and he, too, would be fed raw food. I looked sadly at the huge bag of kibble, with the healthy yellow Lab pictured on it, and the cans of Alpo with gravy, which I had purchased to make the kibble more palatable for Cory, remembering how much I had believed it was the best I could be feeding him.

CHAPTER 18

CORY TRIES BARF

🐾 But I couldn't actually "give my dog a bone" without the OK of a veterinarian. At that time feeding bones to a dog was unheard of. Cory's regular vet called the idea extremely dangerous and recommended that we keep him on the "high quality" kibble he was on and that we start him on Phenobarbital.

I had learned about the terms "kindling" and "mirroring," where the brain starts to teach itself to have seizures because epileptic neurons in the brain "recruit" normal neurons (think about the evil empire winning soldiers over to its side because it can pay them more money than the empire of truth and light), which actually enlarges the area on the one side of the brain that can produce seizures. Then the affected side of the brain mirrors this knowledge to the other side of the brain. In time, the previously healthy side of the brain becomes able to cause seizure activity by itself, so you have both sides of the brain giving out the signals to cause seizures. This knowledge gave me a heightened sense of urgency to do something for Cory.

I studied the yellow pages of the telephone book and located a holistic vet whose practice was on Mercer Island, which is not far from where we live. I called and made our first appointment. She examined Cory and did her own full work-up on him to rule out any possible physical conditions that could be causing his seizures, and she started him on homeopathy. She told me exactly how to feed him a raw, natural, species-appropriate diet, which is widely known among raw feeders as "BARF," which is an acronym for "bones and raw food" or "biologically appropriate raw food." The first time I gave Cory a chicken wing, I felt a curious mixture of doubt and hope. At least if he choked and his eyes bugged out, I would have the benefit of a veterinarian with a medical degree supporting me in doing something so far out of my realm of comfort.

Of course, he loved it, wagging his tail in delight and munching and crunching with a big smile on his face. Feeling somewhat emboldened, I fed him chicken backs with the organs still attached and chicken necks for dinner that night.

We had intended to breed Cory one day, but the vet told us that epilepsy might be an inherited condition, so that option was absolutely eliminated. I reluctantly made the appointment to get him neutered, and I had his teeth cleaned while he was under the anesthesia. That was the last time he needed to have his teeth cleaned because eating raw bones naturally keeps a dog's teeth clean and free of bacteria-laden plaque.

I have come to learn that periodontal disease is the most commonly diagnosed problem in dogs and cats. By the age of two, over 80 percent of dogs and 70 percent of cats have some form of periodontal disease, which can lead to a systemic dysfunction of all other functions in the body. Periodontal disease has been linked to strokes, kidney disease, diabetes, and other life-threatening disorders. Unhealthy teeth and gums in a dog indicate a weakened natural immune system in the animal, and he cannot fight disease as well as he otherwise could.

Before the change in diet, I had bought Cory the recommended doggie toothbrush and dental paste, but they did absolutely nothing in terms of getting the plaque caused from eating kibble and canned food off his teeth. Plaque was winning the battle until Cory started eating raw meat with consumable bones. I learned that raw meat and bones do not allow for plaque to build up. The crunching of the small bones by the dog naturally provides the scraping of the teeth, much as you get when you go to your dentist to have your teeth cleaned. Kibble and canned dog food, no matter what the bag says to the contrary, consists of highly processed food with added fat and preservatives, which will cause plaque.

Even people who have become comfortable with feeding a raw diet to their dogs may still have problems with their gums and teeth because of the treats that they choose to feed them. Often people do not realize that most commercial dog treats (or training treats) contain the flour and sugars that can lead to plaque build-up.

We also learned about ocular compression, where you basically interrupt the electrical malfunction in the brain by applying gentle pressure with the heels of your hands against the dog's closed eyes for about ten seconds on and ten seconds off. This triggers the vagus nerve in the brain that runs through the face, neck, and chest to the lower belly of the dog. We saw time and time again how application of ocular compression helped bring Cory out of a seizure or reduce the intensity of a seizure.

After a seizure, the post ictal phase would often result in a mood change (such as depression), exhaustion, or even blacking out. For some dogs with epilepsy, this phase can last as long as a day. For Cory, it never lasted longer than two hours.

Once Cory starting having frequent seizures, I had to move through the denial, which I had put up as a defense after Cory's first few seizures, where I told myself he was just extra sensitive to something he had eaten or he had just over-exerted himself. Once I could no longer live in that merciful state of denial, my mood switched quickly to depression, where I felt as if the life we had envisioned with Cory was not to be because our most enjoyable activities together would always be compromised. How could I take him to an off-leash park without someone with me to protect him during a seizure? How could we go on a hike when he might go into cluster seizures and need medical intervention quickly? I kept the phone number and directions to the twenty-four-hour emergency veterinary clinic taped to the outside of our kitchen cupboard, but what good would that do if we were out camping?

I had difficulty moving through this period of fear and darkness, but I received help from the support of the owners of epileptic dogs on the canine epilepsy Web site, as well as Cory's vet, who gave us syringes full of Valium to be used rectally if Cory had a seizure that he could not come out of on our camping trips, or even, if he had cluster seizures. My feelings of vulnerability eventually led me to pray for and actually find guidance. The more I empowered myself with knowledge about what people were doing for their epileptic dogs that had positive outcomes, the more I came to understand that Cory was not a cripple in need of my tears but rather a marvelous and beautiful Labrador retriever that could do anything any healthy dog could do, as long as we educated and prepared ourselves to help him to the best of our abilities. I found, as my depression lifted, that I actually had established an incredibly strong psychic bond with Cory; I could see that he understood how much I wanted to help him.

CHAPTER 19

THE RIGHT VETERINARIAN

We took Cory to our neighborhood veterinarian when we first got him for his routine vaccinations and to get his milk teeth pulled (they didn't fall out on their own). Once his seizures started coming more frequently, we had the veterinarian do a full work-up on Cory to see if there could possibly be a medical condition that would respond to treatment. The test results came back negative. Although he had other epileptic patients, Cory's vet did not have any ideas as to what we could do to help him, other than to try the anti-epileptic drugs that were available. At first I was eager to get Cory started on them, but through the process of educating myself, I read with growing alarm that liver damage is a common side-effect of Phenobarbital, with the degree of damage relating to the amount of the drug that needs to be given to the dog to control the seizures. Further, a dog on Phenobarbital must have periodic liver tests done to see if it is being damaged, as well as bile acid tests every three to four months. All of these tests involve drawing blood, and the bile acid test must be done after fasting. I thought about all those trips Cory would have to take to the vet and all those needles poking him to draw his blood. But the worst thing to me was the reports from all the owners of epileptic dogs who opted for this medication telling about how the personalities of their dogs changed so that many of them became lazy, unco-ordinated, weak, lethargic, and overweight. I also learned that Phenobarbital can interfere with a dog's basic thyroid function.

The other anti-epileptic drug of favor at that time was Potassium Bromide, a drug originally used to treat epilepsy in humans. This was the drug of choice to start if you had enough time because it takes longer (usually several months) to reach therapeutic levels in the blood. There is a fine balancing act to get the dosage right with this drug because the drug is affected by the chloride (salt) content of the dog's diet, which could lead to the seizure threshold being lowered. Further, the side-effects of this drug include loss of coordination, muscle pain, stupor, lethargy, and an increase in thirst and hunger. Since Labrador retrievers are already known for their voracious appetites, I could just see what a butterball my uncoordinated, sleepy, starving Cory could easily become.

Many dogs on the canine epilepsy list were on both drugs because of the frequency and severity of their seizures. I read as much as I could and listened to what other people were saying as they started their dogs on one or both of these medications. I kept a journal of those reported experiences so when the day came where we had to make that decision for Cory, we would be as educated as possible about the benefits, risks, and potential personality changes that the drugs could affect.

When we did find the right veterinarian for Cory, she not only gave him custom formulated homeopathic remedies and encouraged us to feed him the raw diet, but she also armed me with syringes filled with Valium, which gave us the peace of mind in bringing Cory with us on camping trips. Although Cory did have many seizures when we were out camping, we never had to use the Valium, although I continued to get a new syringe filled with a fresh dose at every one of his annual visits, even four years after his last seizure.

Chapter 20

Cory Gets a Life Jacket

Cory had a few mild seizures during those first few months on BARF, but they were nothing like the first ones. I started using Rescue Remedy during a seizure, and I saw that they were much milder when I did so. He had a total of four seizures from the time we started him on homeopathy and the raw diet, and then for eleven blissful months he had no more. In those eleven months, I felt that we had conquered the "monster." I forgot about how your heart physically hurts as you have to watch your beloved dog twitch and writhe as if possessed by demons, and all you can do is stand helplessly by. It is amazing how we seem to have our brains wired to forget pain, either emotional or physical, and the longer the time in which everything is normal, the more our minds can create a kind of illusion where we convince ourselves that whatever has hurt us was never really that bad, in retrospect. That is certainly what had happened to me, with the passage of those eleven seizure-free months.

I was one of the people on the canine-epilepsy Web site posting about the tremendous success Cory had achieved with the natural remedies and raw diet. Then, one day in late June of 2003, eleven months after his previous one, Cory had a seizure after strenuous swimming in a lake where we had been throwing a tennis ball for him for several hours. He was not yet out of the lake when he had the seizure, and I got to him first and held his head out of the water until it was over. Cory's seizures almost always came on without warning. If this seizure had happened just a minute before, when he was in a deeper part of the lake, he most certainly would have drowned. I felt responsible for putting Cory in that dangerous situation, and I allowed the shock of it to sink me into a place of self-loathing and anxiety, which weighed on me for a very long time.

This was a clear wake-up call to us that Cory was not cured of his epilepsy and that for the rest of his life he would need a special canine life jacket whenever he swam. I ordered one the moment we got home, and he has worn it ever since when we are around the water. A lot of people have commented over the years on it, and many have questioned why such a strong swimmer would need a life jacket. It has certainly been a good conversation starter over the years. Cory has learned to love it because, when he sees me get it out, it means he gets to go swimming! It puts me at ease because I know, if Cory has a seizure, any one of us can get to him and hold his head out of the water by grabbing the strap attached to the top of it while the life-jacket keeps his body afloat; although Cory never has had a seizure while swimming with his life jacket.

CHAPTER 21

THE ELK AND COYOTES

We have returned again and again to Rimrock Lake in Eastern Washington, where Cory had that unusual episode that turned out to be his first seizure. Although there is no established campground, people often set up camp in the area because it is so beautiful. By the time we arrived on this particular trip, the sun had gone down, and already pitch black surrounded us. We were glad we knew the area well enough to know where to park.

Jay went about preparations to build a campfire while Cory and I went down in the area where the lake usually was. It is a reservoir lake, controlled by a dam, and sometimes the lake is drained to provide water for nearby farms. There was no moon out that night, and not a cloud in the sky. I love to look at stars and identify constellations, so I grabbed my glow-in-the dark star charts and headed down into the crater. It was a peaceful scene to be in the middle of where the lake used to be, with Cory running around me and Jay up on the bank sitting next to the fire. We had the entire lake all to ourselves that evening. Occasionally, I could hear Cory sloshing through water, and I wondered what could he be getting into. He loved running around as much as I loved sitting there delighting in the starlight.

When I got tired enough to head back to the campfire, Cory followed me close behind. As the fire died, Jay and I talked about how fortunate we were to be living in such a beautiful state and how much we loved sharing this extraordinary life we were having together. We turned in eventually and started to fall asleep in our bed while Cory, who sleeps on the floor in our motor home on a down comforter, did the same. Suddenly the sound of elk bugling filled the air, following by the high-pitched yipping of a pack of coyotes. The elk noise turned into elk screams, and the coyotes were yipping and howling with the delight of a group attack. The next thing I knew, Cory had seemingly levitated off the floor, landed on our bed, and dived into our double-wide sleeping bag, scooting all the way down to our feet. He had never shown any fear of any kind before, and we started laughing so hard I thought my sides would burst, as Cory quivered quietly in his hiding place.

Eventually the commotion stopped, and we all fell asleep. The next morning, Cory and I stepped out of the motor home to a most glorious sight! A big river was running the entire length of the lake basin, although it was shallow and fairly wide in some places. The morning sun was already over the horizon and glinting off the water, tossing diamonds casually here and there. So that's what Cory had been into the night before! He looked at me in confirmation of our mutual delight, and we headed down the hill to explore the river. We found that it was teeming with spawning kokanee. Cory had fun running into the river to chase the fish, and we walked along it for about a half mile before I decided to go back and let Jay in on the discovery.

That weekend was memorable not just because of the elk, coyotes, and river filled with fish, but also because the three of us got to experience it privately, which allowed us to see wildlife we would not have if other people had been around. To our amazement, a family of wild turkeys actually walked through our camp, seemingly unfazed by our presence, while Cory was down in the lake crater, playing in the river. It was October but unseasonably warm during the day yet cold at night. The crisp weather had set the maples ablaze in fall colors of scarlet and yellow, as spectacular as an oil painting. It was too beautiful to leave so we drove to the nearest pay phone and informed our respective offices we were playing hooky for another night. Altogether we sighted fourteen different fauna on that trip. The list of animals that we saw in those two days included birds such as eagles, hawks, and osprey, feeding on the dying fish. We also watched chipmunks, squirrels, coyotes, elk, and deer, and, most remarkably, the turkeys which we have never otherwise seen in our twenty-five years of camping together.

CHAPTER 22

LEMON

In addition to stealing food at every opportunity, Cory had another bad habit in not readily dropping a ball or stick during a game of fetch. He loved to retrieve the toy and then run around as if to say, "Hey, guys, look at me!" which isn't so much fun if you are the human element in the game. Again, thanks to research on the Internet (my previous provider of the helpful mousetrap information), I got the idea to squirt lemon juice into Cory's mouth. I bought one of those little yellow squeeze things at the grocery store which are shaped like lemons and filled with lemon juice, and the next time Cory played the keep-away game that I wanted to be the fetch-and-retrieve game, I snagged Cory, snapped on his leash, and sternly said "**LEMON**," and then proceeded to squirt the juice into Cory's mouth, which by the way was still housing the tennis ball. He dropped the ball instantly and did everything he could to get the awful taste out of his mouth. He obviously really hated it. We may have needed to use it one or two more times in his life, but for the most part all we need to do is say "lemon," and he will drop whatever is in his mouth like a marine snapping to attention for an officer.

One afternoon, I was watching over the dinner I was cooking outdoors in my Dutch oven while we were camping at Lake Kachess. I had Cory on my radar and knew he had gone around to the other side of the lake to get some children to engage in a game of fetch with him. The lake has mountains on all sides around it, which can create interesting acoustics. I looked up to see a little girl huff-puffing her way over to me, with her cheeks flushed and her eyes bright. I asked her what was wrong, and she said my dog wasn't playing fair and wouldn't drop the stick she wanted to throw for him, so I told her to go back to where Cory and the other children were and to say "Cory, LEMON," to him. When she returned to that place I heard all of the children cry out together "**CORY, LEMON,**" and it echoed off the canyon walls, "lemon, *mon, mon, mon.*" Cory did drop the stick but then tucked his tail between his legs and trotted back to me, looking quite unhappy about the mountain gods that had interrupted his fun with the kids.

CHAPTER 23

MERLIN

With the passage of years, Cory eventually would tire out, and we began to notice that when we would throw a ball or stick for him he would suffer with aches and pains afterwards. Since homeopathy had worked well for us before, I bought a new homeopathic remedy called "ArnicAid" at the grocery store. It contains Arnica Montana, which is for muscle strains and helps with pain, generally. Within minutes of receiving it, Cory would always get complete relief and be ready for more fun and activity. Although his spirit was certainly willing and he had plenty of energy, we could see that too much intensity just wasn't good for Cory's body, so when he was about eight years old, we taught him to "self-swim."

This meant that Cory would go into the water (with his life jacket on, of course), and we would not throw anything.

Eventually he would get bored with us and start looking into the water and become interested in all the rocks on the lake floor and the tiny silver minnows that would tickle at his paws, and he would thoroughly enjoy himself on his own. This was actually a wonderful phase of our lives because Cory was peaceful and engaged and getting appropriate exercise and we were no longer on the spot to have to throw the ball or stick over and over. Before this happy time, I actually injured my right elbow from throwing a ball so much, and it hurt for well over a year.

In the summer of Cory's tenth year, we were camping at one of our favorite lakes, in a campground. We had arrived the day before and walked up to the place in the campground reserved for the summer hosts, and we exchanged hellos with the couple who were the hosts for that summer, and we met their canine companions. One of them, Merlin, hit it off right away with Cory. It might have been because they were the same age and about the same height and weight, but they also had great mutual respect for each other. They sniffed noses curiously and visibly relaxed with each other.

The next morning, Cory and I went out for our morning walk, and I noticed the camp hostess, sitting under a tree with Merlin lying beside her. I called out a cheery "Good morning," and she did not respond. So I asked if everything was OK, and she said, "No, my baby is dying." Cory and I walked over to them, and it was clear that Merlin was seriously ill. She said that Merlin had been extremely sick all night long, and that morning, just as the sun was slipping over the horizon, he got up and walked to the tree, which was right beside the lake, and he lay down there, as if he knew he did not have much longer and he wanted to look at the lake in the time he had left.

I murmured to Cory to go self-swim, and he slipped into the lake and began swimming long, slow, lazy circles while Merlin watched him. I sat with Merlin and his guardian and listened as she told me the story of his wonderful life and how she had been with him since he was a puppy no older than Cory was when we got him. I cried with her and offered what meager comfort I could while Cory continued to swim so gracefully he didn't make any noise whatsoever. I believe we had spent about an hour with them when I felt that the time must be very near, and I wanted them to have that moment when Merlin's spirit left his body to be private for them. So I said as softly as a whisper, "Cory, let's go," and without a second's hesitation, Cory walked out of the lake, and he and I returned to the motor home to tell Jay about our extraordinary morning.

When the three of us returned to the spot, Merlin's body was still there. His owner had gone back to their RV to get assistance from her husband to move him. We waited there to keep wild animals and insects away until they returned with a large blanket. Jay and I helped move Merlin onto the blanket and then into the back of a truck. As sad as that day was, I was so blessed to have been a part of it. There was a magicality about that event that made me physically feel the intense connection of all life, coordinated by a dog with a magician's name. Cory's behavior was nothing short of extraordinary. He seemed to understand what was happening, and he showed reverence and respect that made me proud. I also believe that Cory and I were meant to appear in Merlin's life when we did and that Merlin had chosen Cory and me the day before to give comfort and support to the beloved humans he would soon leave. He also loved having his life's story told while he could still hear it, and that is exactly what I will do for Cory when this story is finished.

This is the place which Merlin chose as his final resting place.

CHAPTER 24

JAYSON LEAVES HOME

Cory and Jayson slept in the bed together since the day Cory became house-trained. The two of them acted more like brothers than best friends. When traveling together, Jayson would complain loudly that Cory was breathing too hard or drooling or hogging space, treating him like a typical annoying/loved sibling. Cory clearly worshipped Jayson and did not like to be out of his presence. Those weeks which Jayson spent at summer camps over the years were hard for Cory. And then when Jayson left home to go to college, Cory had an even harder time adjusting. Used to sleeping on Jayson's bed every night with him, he tried sleeping there alone but gave it up quickly and decided that the couch in our living room was a better fit, I think because he can feel the sides around him and he can pretend his back is up against Jayson's. It was a big adjustment for all of us, but I think hardest of all for Cory. I could see that Cory was lonely for his boy so I hired a dog walker to come and get him two to four times a week and take him to our local off-leash dog park where Cory would spend several hours chasing tennis balls. For some reason, most of the other dogs love to chase Cory. Cory doesn't mind them, but he has never shown much interest in dogs, focusing, instead, on children and anything he could fetch and retrieve. We had to give up the off-leash park when Cory turned eleven years old because he just started getting too worn out and sore and could not get back in the truck. He still dreams about chasing those tennis balls, though, and paddles his legs in his sleep with a big grin on his face.

Over time Jayson picked up guitar playing and would often play songs for us in our home as well as in the light of many a campfire. Not to be outdone, Cory always would go and get a squeaky toy, which he "played" with energy while lying at Jayson's feet. So, as Jayson played and sang for us, Cory provided the rhythmic squeaking to accompany him, which was often quite strangely spot on.

CHAPTER 25

CONCLUSION

Cory's last seizure on May 22, 2005 came one day after his eighth birthday. Somewhere along the way, he developed a mild thyroid imbalance, for which he now gets thyroid medication. We do know that the thyroid condition is not what caused his seizures because of the full work-ups done by two different veterinarians earlier in his life. By the time of his last seizure, Cory had been on the strictly raw diet for four years. Although it took time for his system to get healthy enough to overcome whatever had caused the seizures, he did it without any anti-epileptic drugs, which is the miracle of this story. I do not mean in any way to say that anti-epileptic drugs are bad because, in many cases, they make the difference between life and death. It is just that, for Cory, we got the chance to show the world that in some fortunate cases there are other options.

I attribute our success to feeding Cory a raw, natural diet, the way God intended dogs to eat. For years, I was the "hunter," bringing the dead chicken, game hen, rabbit, or other small prey parts home from the grocery store and sorting them into small meals to be wrapped and frozen. We bought Cory his own small freezer so we didn't have to make daily "hunting" trips. I bought green, leafy vegetables, such as collard greens, and would pulp them in the blender with other veggies, such as cucumbers, zucchini, carrots, parsley, and whatever else looked good, and then pour the resultant green slop into freezer containers. I would add about a quarter cup of the thawed veggie slop to the chicken parts to ensure that Cory really did get 100 percent of his nutritional daily needs. A few years ago, I became aware of a local company that makes the meals with organic meat and vegetables, and they deliver the frozen packages right to my door. This ensures that Cory gets a nice variety of meats, and it is all grain-free, raw, organic meat with bones.

My research and personal experience have led me to believe that commercial dog food is inadvertently poisoning our dogs. I believe that it is directly causing all kinds of illnesses in dogs, including cancer. If changing a dog's diet to a species-appropriate one can reduce or even eliminate epileptic seizures, imagine how much healthy dogs could benefit from eating this way!

I return in my mind to that glorious day in late July of 2000 and am filled with a sense of awe at all we have learned on this ten-year journey. I have already booked our camping reservations throughout the coming summer. As of last summer, Cory needs to use a ramp to get in and out of the motor home.

He gives grumpy little grrrs from time to time as he adjusts his position to try to get more comfortable. But he still has a keen sense of sight and hearing, and he can enjoy the mountain lakes and rivers with us, even if we all now must experience them in a less energetic way than we did years before.

As I write these last words, Cory lies beside me, perhaps reading my thoughts and seeing the images in my mind of the lake that was so sparkly emerald green beneath the shadow of Mt. Adams. He does not recall any of the drama of that day. He is wagging his tail, his gaze on me expectant, as if to say ... "I'm ready when you are!"